Traveling Adventures

A Traveler's Record Book

havoc
PUBLISHING

© 1997 Havoc Publishing

ISBN 1-57977-103-3

Published and created by Havoc Publishing

San Diego, California

First Printing, May 1997

Designed by Juddesign

Some images © 1997 PhotoDisc, Inc.

Printed in China

Please write to us for more information on our
Havoc Publishing Record Books and Products.

HAVOC PUBLISHING

7868 Silverton Avenue, Suite A

San Diego, California 92126

Traveling Adventures

A Traveler's Record Book

A Record Book For

_____

Contents

From Point A to Point B

Points of Departure & Places I've Been

Don't Leave Without It

Packing and Other Tales of Horror

Photographs

Journal Entry

Friends Made Along the Way

Photographs

Places to Hang

The Best Food Ever

Arts & Sightseeing

Totally Entertaining

Photographs

Shopping Adventures

Places to Rest My Head

Contents

Off the Beaten Path

Photographs

Incurable Romantic

Currencies I've Exchanged

Journal Entry

Solitary Places

Unusual Things I Discovered

Photographs

Uncharted Territory

Senses

Lost & Found

Street Scenes & Countrysides

Photographs

More Notes Along the Journey

From Point A

☐ **Road**

☐ **Air**

Departure date:

Left from:

Arrived at:

Departure date:

Left from:

Arrived at:

Departure date:

Left from:

Arrived at:

Departure date:

Left from:

Arrived at:

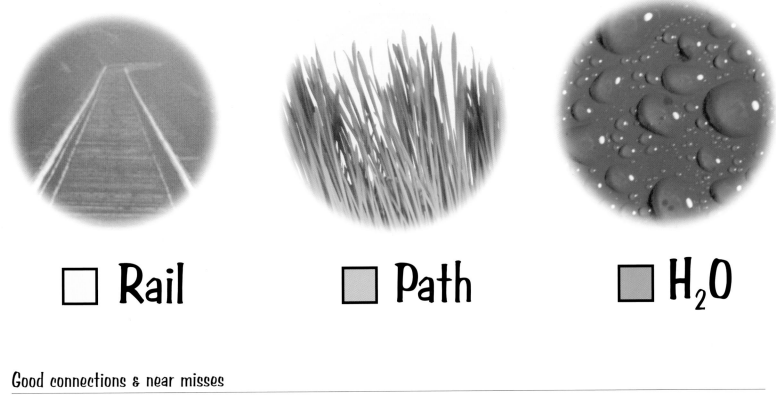

☐ Rail   ☐ Path   ☐ H$_2$O

Good connections & near misses

Longest days of travel

Most connections in one day

Most cities in one day

Most difficult city to get to or through

Easiest city to get to or through

.... To Point B

Points of Departure

Travel companions

Well—traveled routes

Places we blew through

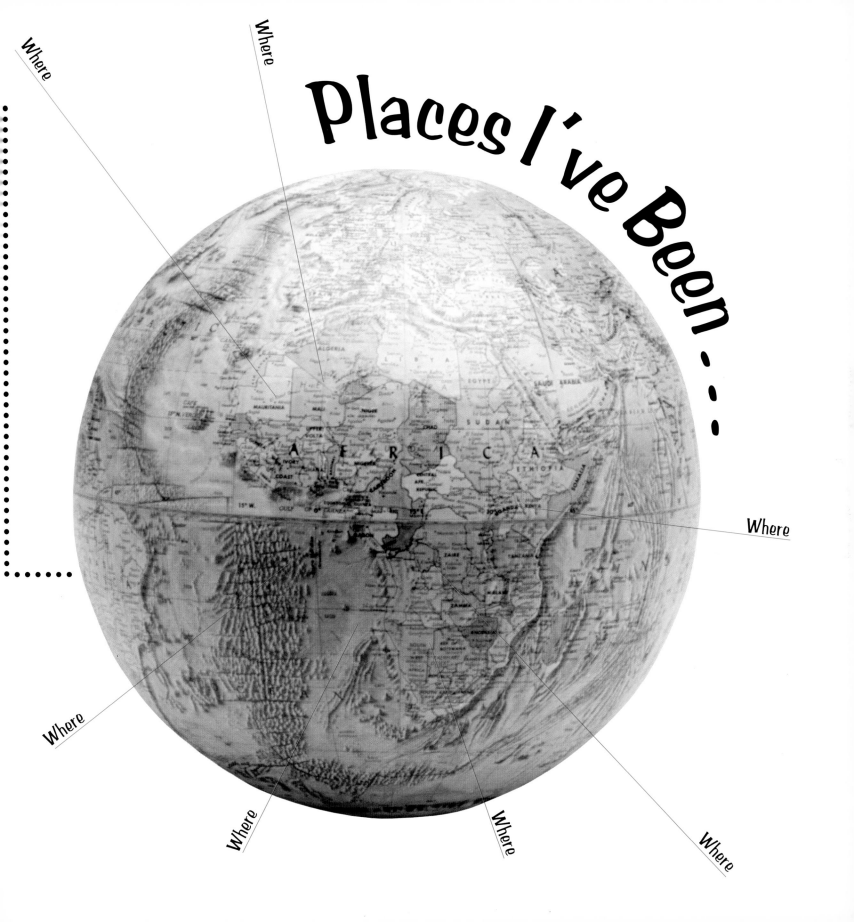

Places I've Been - - -

Where

Where

Where

Where

Where

Where

Where

Where

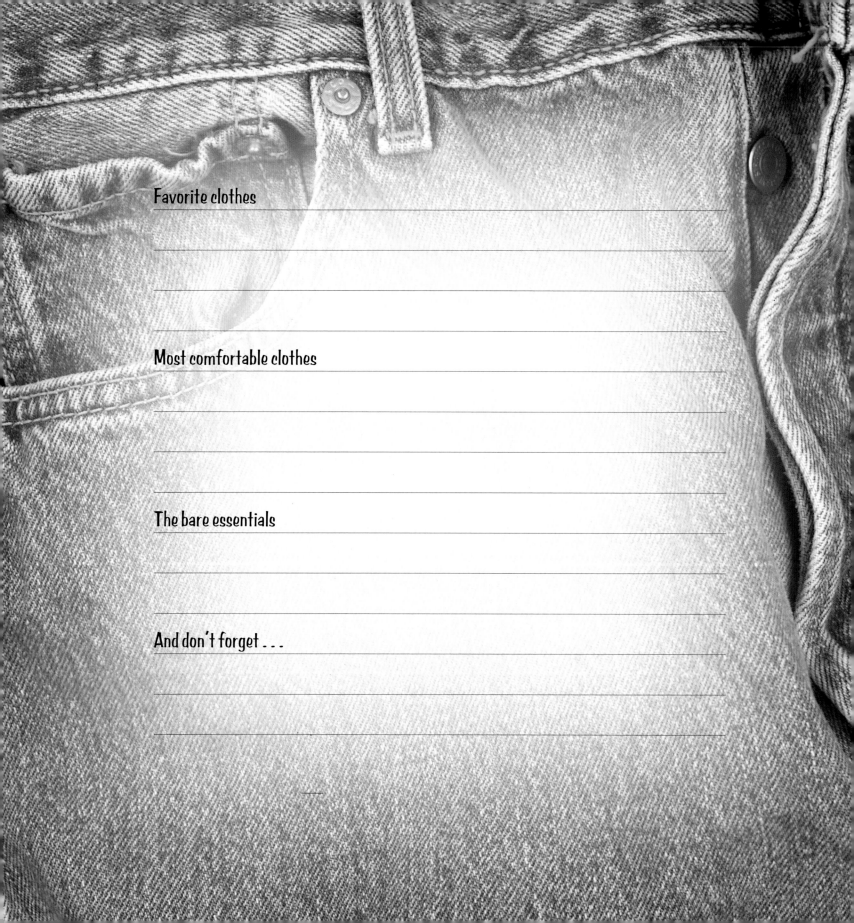

Favorite clothes

_____

_____

_____

_____

Most comfortable clothes

_____

_____

_____

_____

The bare essentials

_____

_____

_____

And don't forget . . .

_____

_____

_____

Don't Leave Without It

Packing and Other Tales of Horror

Long lost luggage

Broken bags

Could've sworn I packed it

This all fit in here yesterday

Messiest travel mate

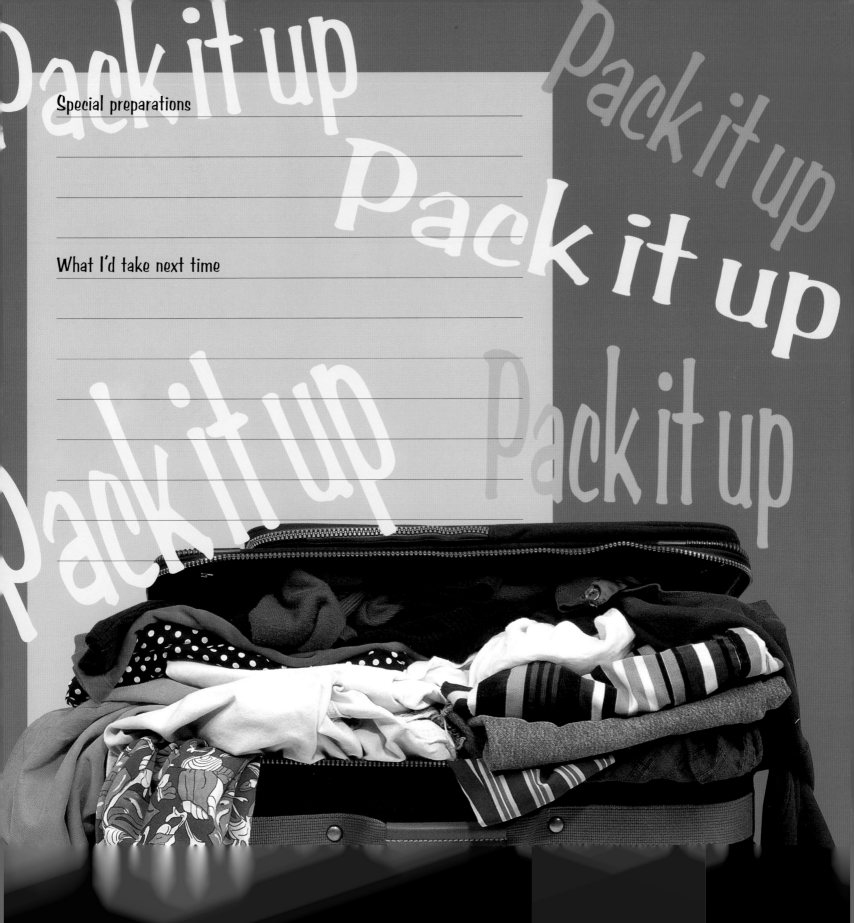

Special preparations

What I'd take next time

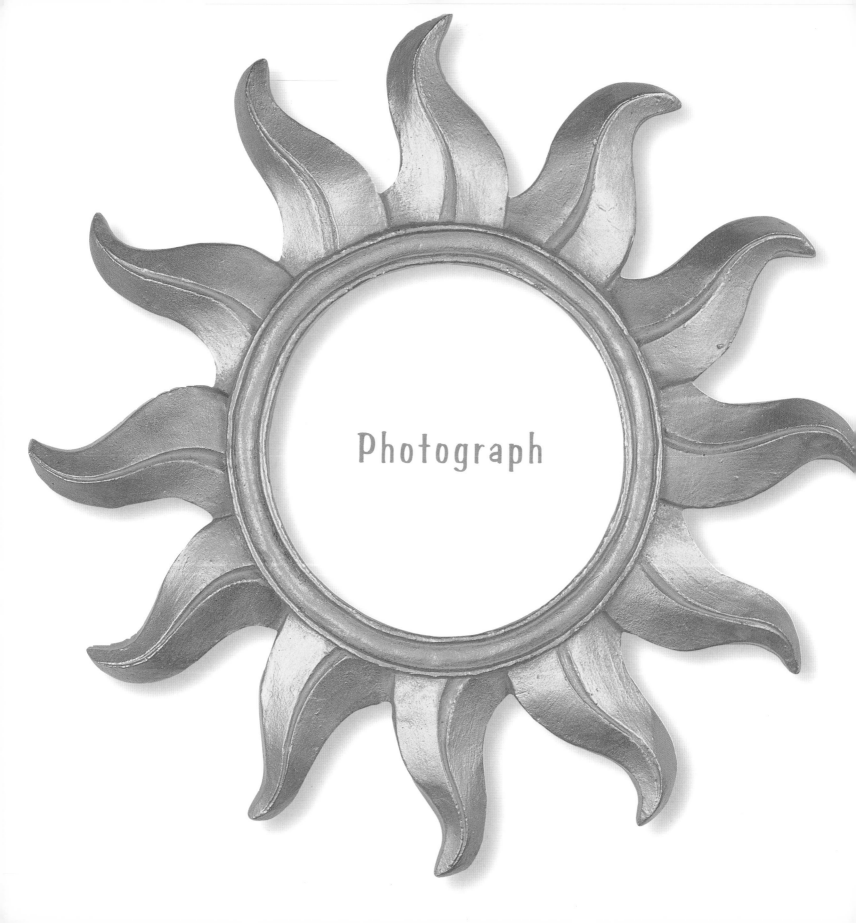

Photograph

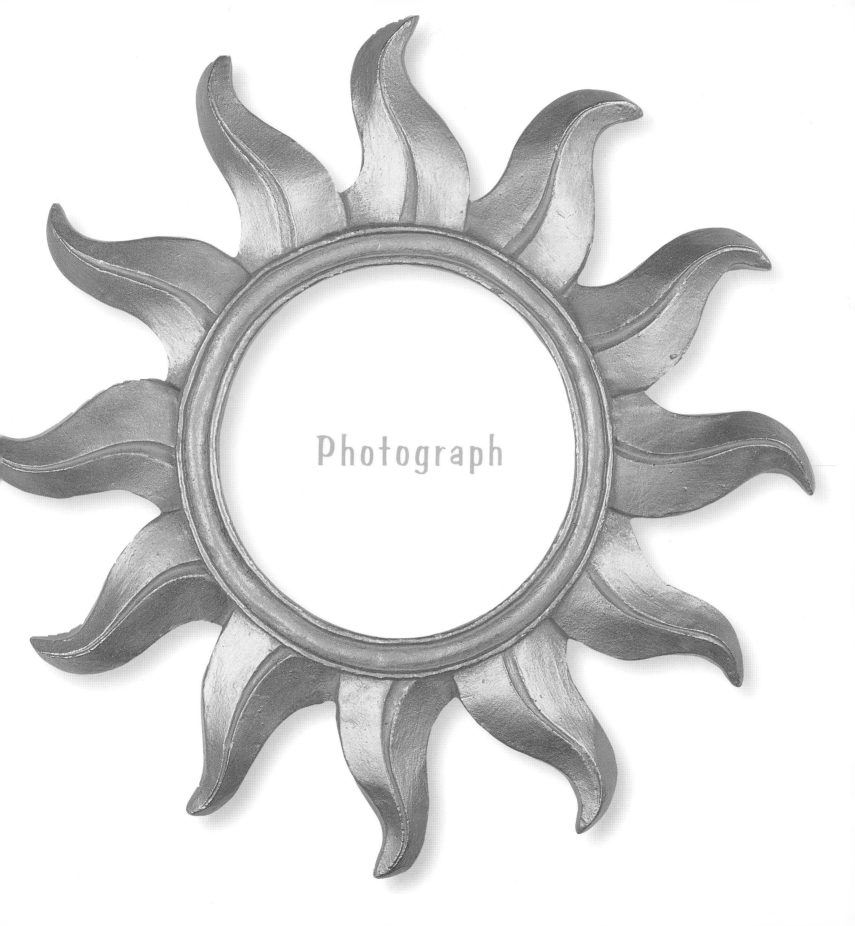

Photograph

Date:

Place:

Journal Entry

Date: _____

Place: _____

_____

_____

_____

_____

_____

_____

_____

_____

_____

_____

_____

_____

Friends Made Along the Way

Name

Address

Telephone   e-mail

Where we met

Name

Address

Telephone   e-mail

Where we met

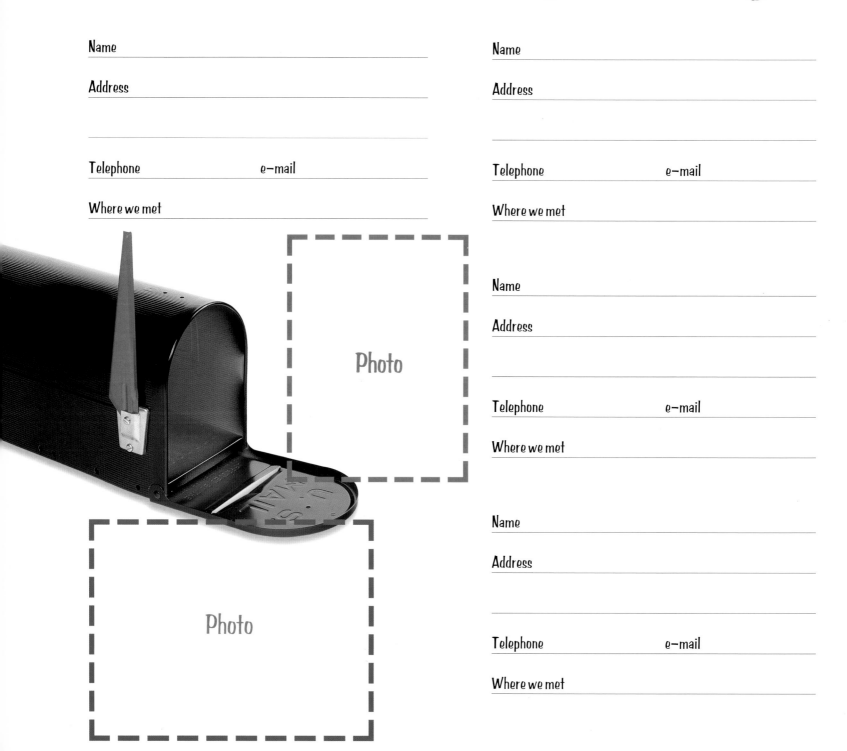

Photo

Name

Address

Telephone   e-mail

Where we met

Photo

Name

Address

Telephone   e-mail

Where we met

...More Friends

Name

Address

Telephone   e-mail

Where we met

Name

Address

Telephone   e-mail

Where we met

Photo

Name

Address

Telephone   e-mail

Where we met

Name

Address

Telephone   e-mail

Where we met

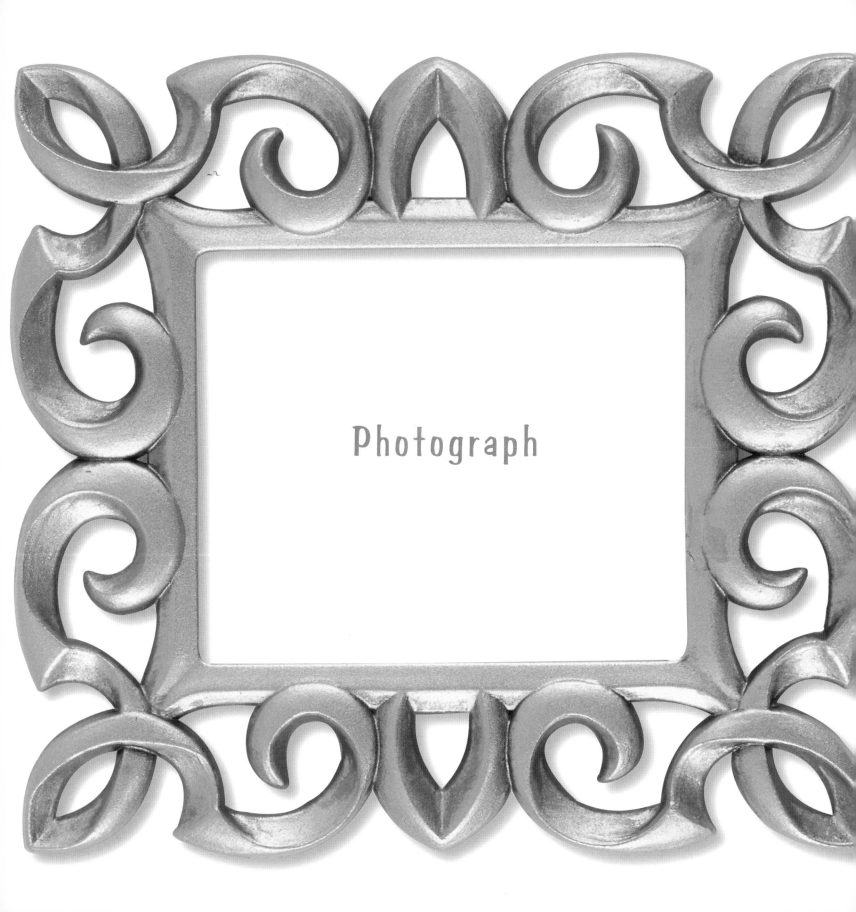

Photograph

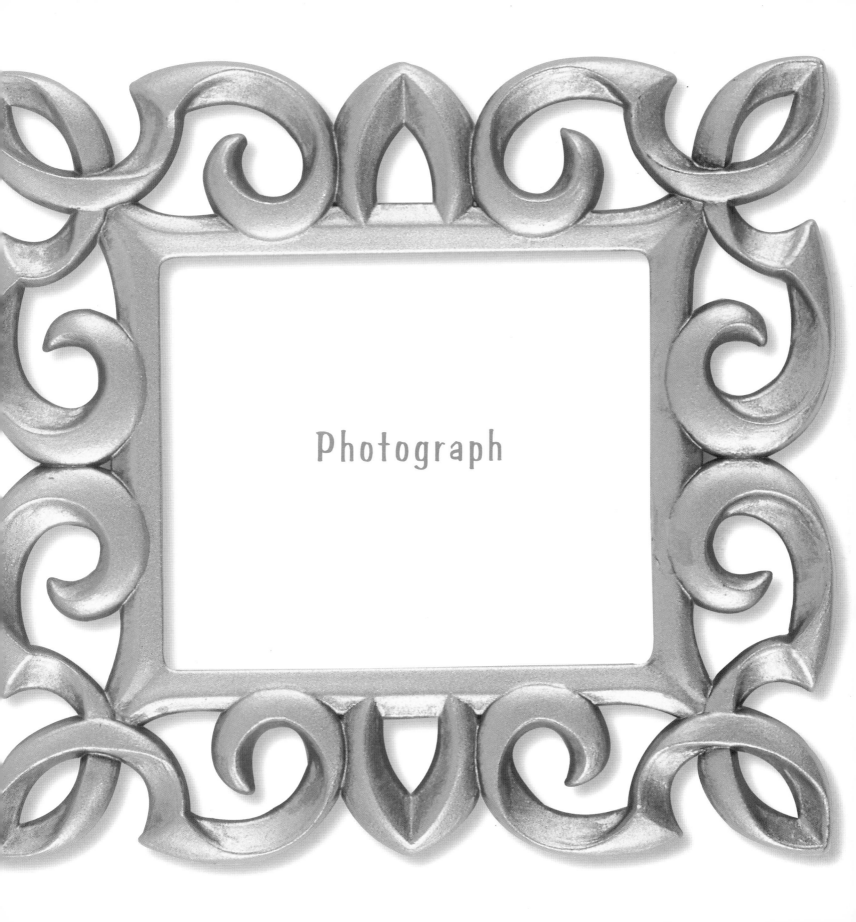

Photograph

I travel for travel's sake. The great affair is to move ~ Robert Louis Stevenson

Places to Hang

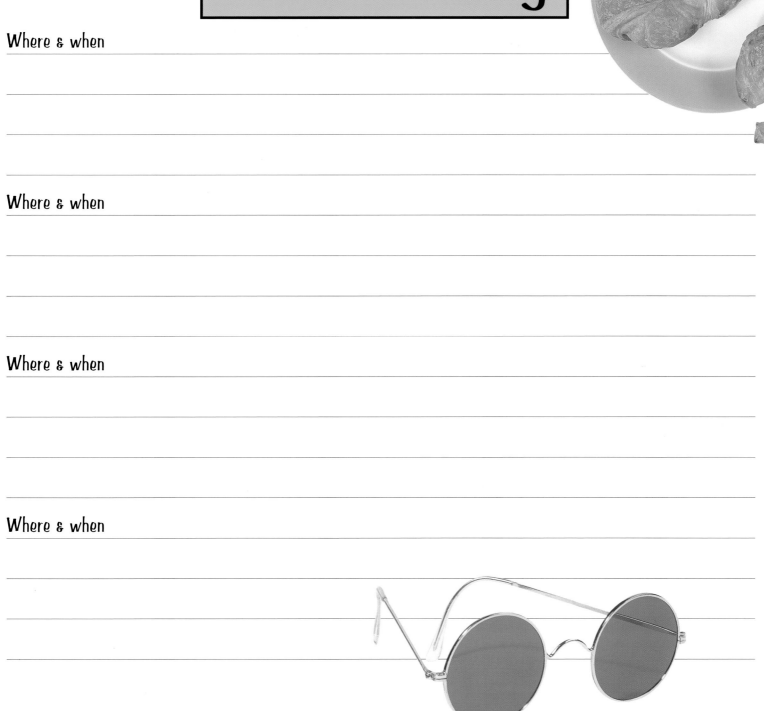

Where & when

_____

_____

_____

Where & when

_____

_____

_____

Where & when

_____

_____

_____

Where & when

_____

_____

_____

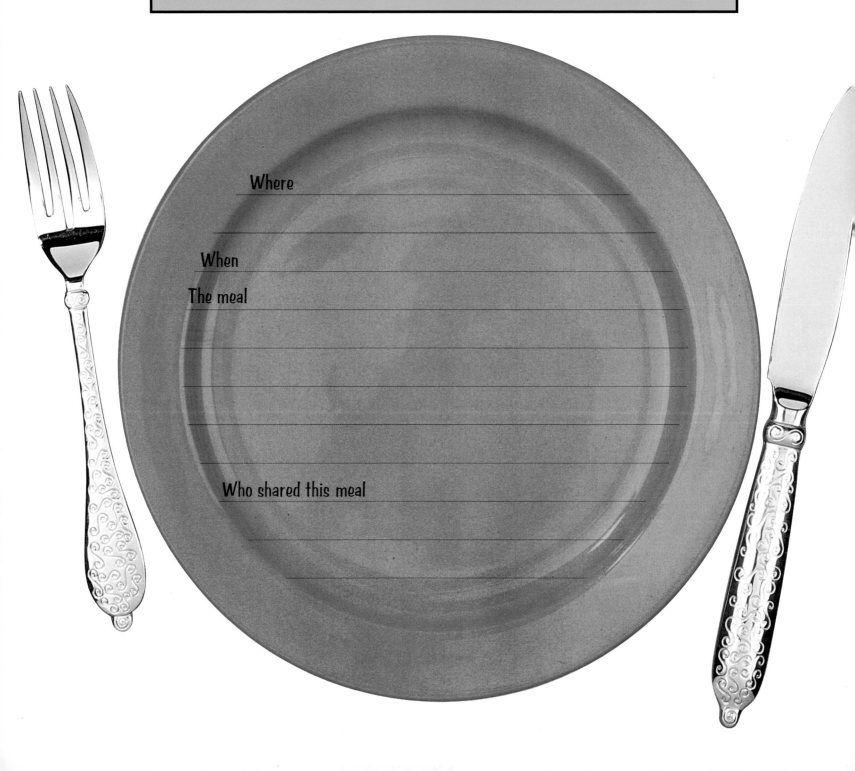

The BEST Food Ever....

Where

When

The meal

Who shared this meal

Favorite Meal

Favorite restaurants

_____
_____
_____
_____
_____
_____
_____

Favorite wines

_____
_____
_____

Favorite dessert

_____
_____
_____

Most adventurous food

_____
_____
_____
_____

WORLD

1995

BARREL AGED

CHARDONNAY

art

Sightseeing

Museums, Landmarks and Architecture

Totally Entertaining

Place your ticket stub here

Place your ticket stub here

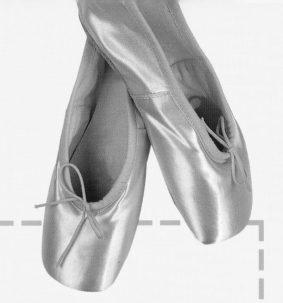

Favorite Theatre & Ballet

_____

_____

_____

_____

_____

Concerts & Other Entertainment

_____

_____

_____

_____

_____

_____

Place your ticket stub here

Place your ticket stub here

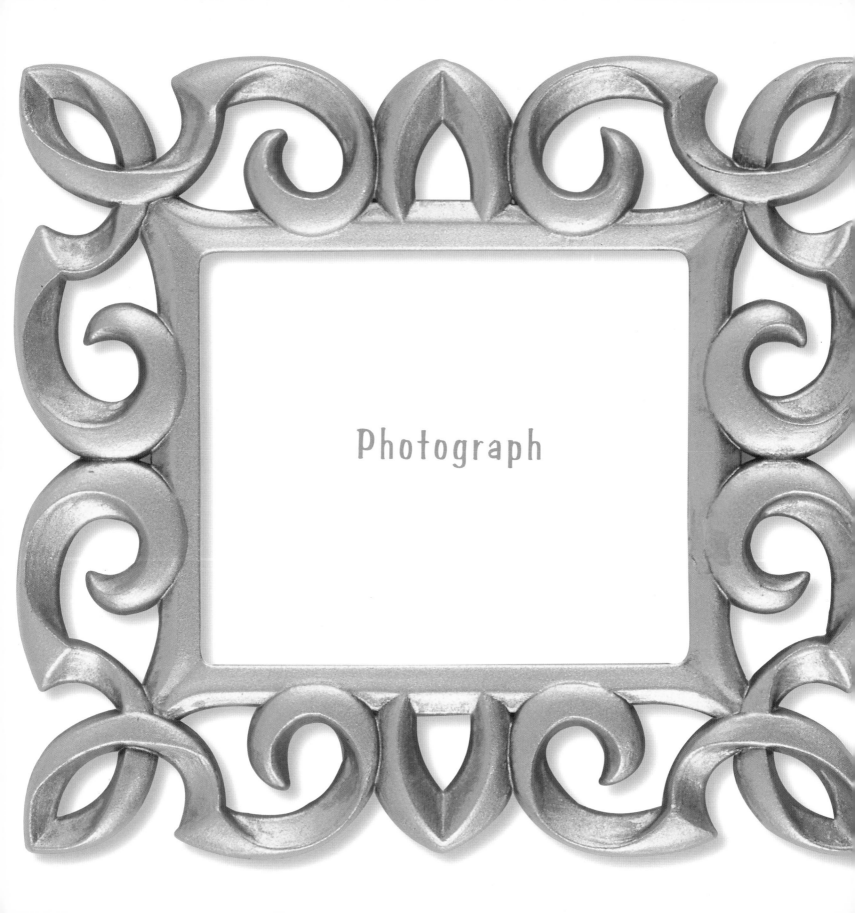

Photograph

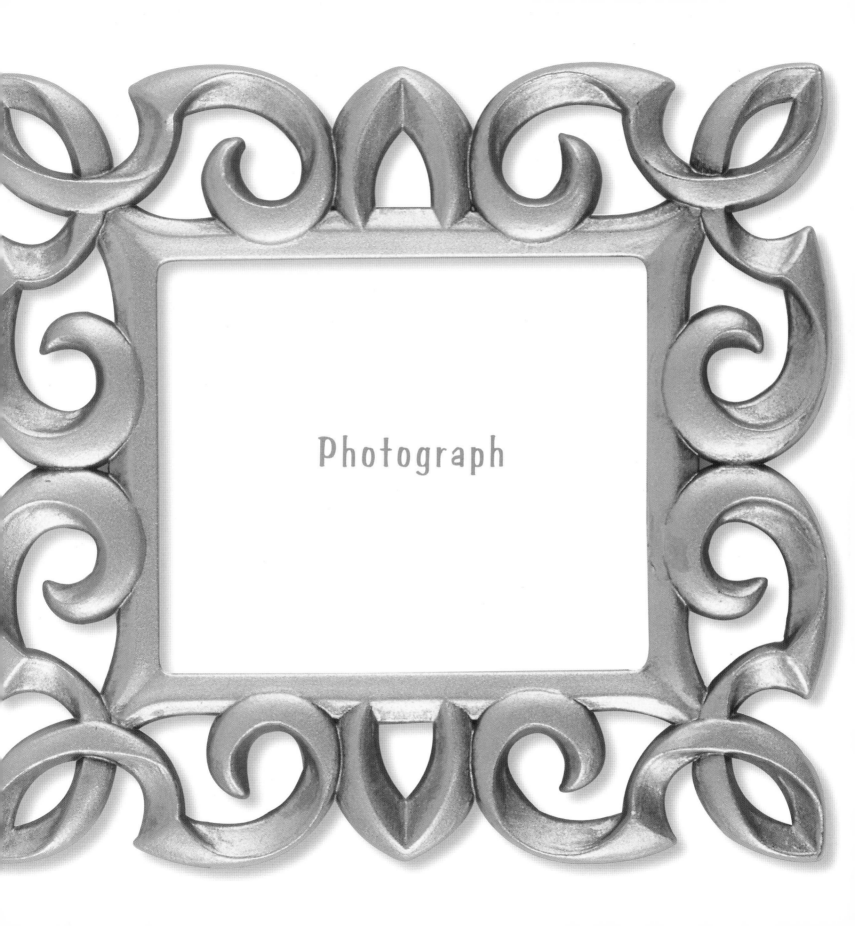

Photograph

Shopping Adventures

Favorite items purchased

Favorite shops and stores

Most expensive item

Most fun shopping

Most adventurous shopping experiences

What was purchased spur of the moment

Most difficult item to bring home

PENSIONE

Hotels
Hotelinns

motel

Bed & Breakfast

Places to Rest My Head

Where & When

Where & When

Where & When

Where & When

Favorite place

Best value

Most expensive

Off the Beaten Path...

adv. phr. Not well known or often used: not gone to or seen by many people; unusual

_____

_____

_____

_____

_____

_____

_____

_____

_____

_____

canyons • hills • early morning treks •

Photograph

Most Romantic Spots...

Most romantic viewpoints

Most romantic restaurants

Most romantic nights

Most romantic days

Most romantic gardens

Incurable Romantic

Most romantic places

Romance languages I did or didn't understand

Wild nights worth writing about

Currencies I've Exchanged

Exchange Rates

Types of Currency

Journal Entry

Date:_____

Place:_____

_____

_____

_____

_____

_____

_____

_____

_____

_____

Journal Entry

Date: _____

Place: _____

_____

_____

_____

_____

_____

_____

_____

_____

_____

Favorite retreats

_____

_____

_____

_____

Favorite weekend getaways

_____

_____

_____

Favorite short trips

_____

_____

_____

Healthiest places I've gone

_____

_____

_____

Solitary Places

Date:

Place:

Date:

Place:

Unusual Things I Discovered

_____
_____
_____
_____
_____
_____
_____
_____
_____
_____
_____
_____
_____

Photograph

Photograph

What am I doing here?

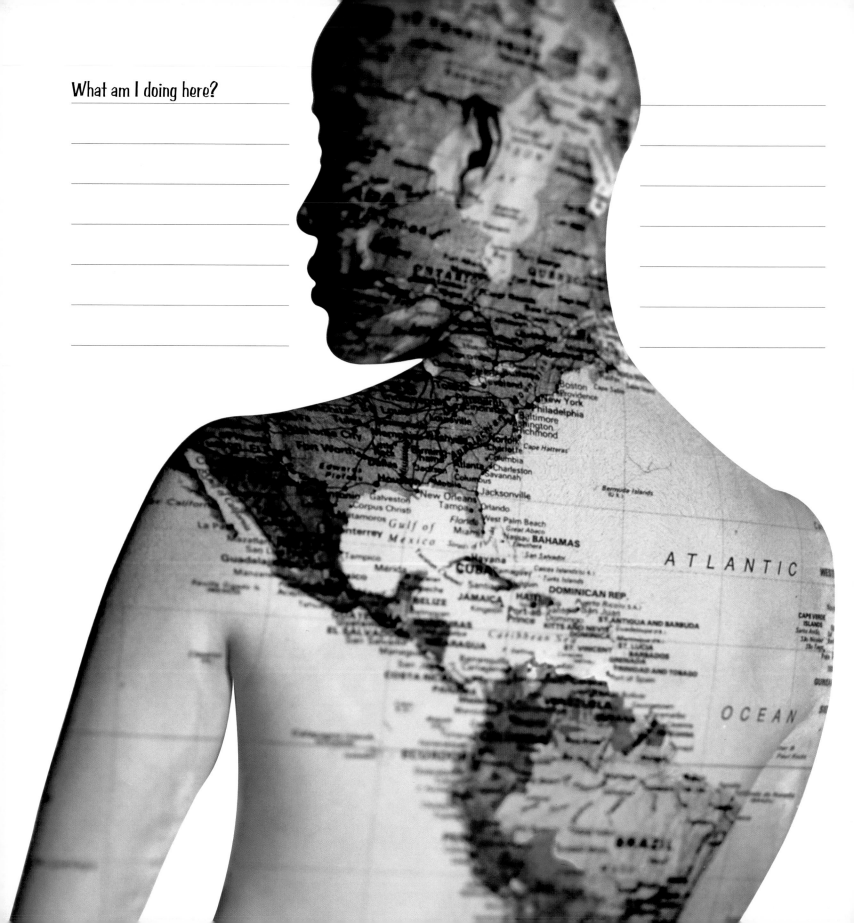

Uncharted Territory

_____

_____

_____

_____

_____

_____

_____

_____

_____

_____

_____

_____

_____

Time Zones

Based on Greenwich Mean Time, London

Anchorage	−10 hours
Buenos Aires	−4 hours
Chicago	−6 hours
Delhi	+5 hours
Honolulu	−11 hours
Hong Kong	+7 hours
London	12 noon
Los Angeles	−8 hours
Mexico City	−7 hours
New York	−5 hours
Rio de Janeiro	−3 hours
Rome	+1 hour
Tokyo	+8 hours
Washington D.C.	−5 hours

SEEN

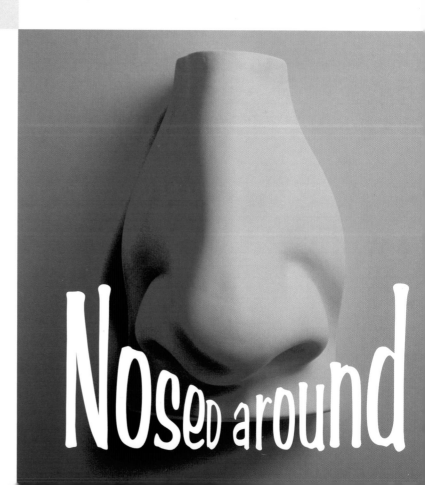

NOSED around

Spoke About

HEARD

Lost

and

Found

_____

_____

_____

_____

_____

_____

_____

_____

_____

_____

Street Scenes

& Countrysides

POPULATION

People 98½

Horses 101

Dogs To Ma

Photograph

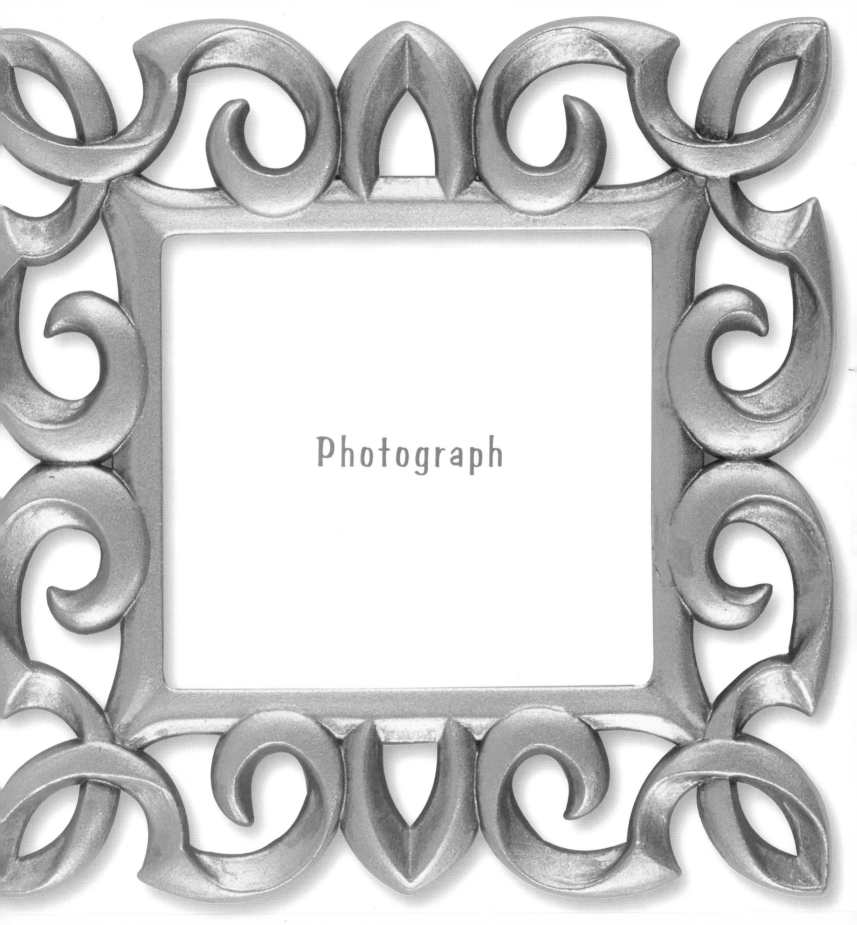

Photograph

More Notes Along the Journey

Available Record Books from Havoc

Animal Antics – Cats

Animal Antics – Dogs

Couples

Girlfriends

Golf

Grandmother

Our Honeymoon

Mom

Sisters

Tying the Knot

Traveling Adventures

Please write to us with your ideas for additional
Havoc Publishing Record Books and Products

HAVOC PUBLISHING

7868 Silverton Avenue, Suite A

San Diego, California 92126